Death and the Good Doctor Whetstone

Sean Lause

Cyberwit.net
HIG 45 Kaushambi Kunj, Kalindipuram
Allahabad - 211011 (U.P.) India
http://www.cyberwit.net
Tel: +(91) 9415091004
E-mail: info@cyberwit.net

Printed at VCORE LLP.

"Every true story ends in death."——Ernest Hemingway

For my son, Christopher, and my brother, Kevin, with love.

Acknowledgements

I would like to thank Tom Beery and Will Wells for all their wise advice as I wrote this book.

These poems from Death and the Good Doctor Whetstone first appeared in the following journals:

"The first hero"————-*Ardent*

"From The Secret Diary of Lucy Westenra"————-*The Roanoke Review*

"36"————-*The Alaska Quarterly, The Saranac Review*

"Plasto Man"———*The Manhattan Review*

"Of a man skating"————-*Lost Lake Folk Opera*

Contents

Part One: Death and the Good Doctor Whetstone 9

Death and the Good Doctor Whetstone 10

Part Two: Youth 25

Memory snake 26
Rock of secrets 27
The forever wound 28
A dead soldier speaks 29
The Witness I 30
The First Hero 32
Dance with dark and light 33
From The Secret Diary of Lucy Westenra 34
House of Dreams and Demons 35
The Girdle 36
Summer of '62 38
The candy apocalypse 40
The cat from Hiroshima 46
Playing fake baseball for keeps 47
Coal cellar 48
Alive in the death cult 49
36 50

Part Three: Age 57

The Giant Pyrfera 58
Night-driving 59
Atropos on Main 60
The white van 61
Dispossessions 62
Insomnia caravan 64
Tower in Winter Woods 66

Dead Guy on a Horse 67
On the day of another American mass-shooting 68
The ant poets 69
The end of nightmares 70
Theomania 71
Such language 73
Hospice 75
The permeability of touch 76
The ancient fishermen 77
Death and only the lonely 78
What I saw at the funeral home 79
Blessing the dead 80
These days 81
Facets of silence and memory 82
Elegy: What holds the eye now is what remembers 83
Plasto Man 84
Of a man skating 85
Enquento 86
Kaleidoscope of mirrors 88
Three times not to die 90
Rules of Retirement 91
It 92
Rain I don't mind 92
Renga in Gold, White, Blue and Green 94
Light and silence 96
Autumn leaving 98
How the moon inhabits time 99

Part One: Death and the Good Doctor Whetstone

Death and the Good Doctor Whetstone

Opening shot: Fade in on a parody of a Nineteenth Century Victorian flat. Soloman Pierce, parody of a world-famous detective, sits in his favorite chair across from his friend and assistant, Dr. Whetstone, smoking a clay pipe. Dr. Whetstone smokes a good cigar. The March Hare sits between then, warming his paws by the fire. Their chairs partly face each other and partly face the audience. In the center of this group is a low table with a chess board, a few bottles of bourbon, scotch and Cointreau, and drinking glasses. Stage left is a parody of a Victorian door made of engraved oak, merely a frame with a door, leading nowhere. Treadwell McPherson, a parody of a Hard-Boiled Detective, paces near them, Bogarting a cigarette. Whetstone stands and confidently strolls towards Treadwell. Their eyes meet. They nod to each other and face the audience.

Whetstone (to audience): Wind and rain thrash at the casements as if man were the sinner and nature the scourge. The four of us sit by Soloman Pierce's fireplace, which as usual on such a night is crackling and bright. We are debating an unsolved crime, one Pierce claims is the most challenging he has ever encountered in all his experience as a consulting detective.

Treadwell (to audience): The night bignowheres alley to alley, drunk on death and silence. Skeleton fire escapes release their shadows that trail us like forgotten sins. We've been here most of the day, drying our hands and paws, bringing new meaning to bupkiss.

(They return to their seats.)

Soloman Pierce: Always begin, Whetstone, by pursuing the vital detail, Le Mot Juste, the one that unlocks a whole story. Pursue that detail all the way to from whence it came, then unlock what it portends.

Treadwell: Portends? Tell me you're wisecracking. It's more than details, Pierce. It's a total situation. The parts are just part of other parts.

Soloman: What say you, Whetstone?

Whetstone: I must admit to being somewhat flummoxed, Pierce. I see both perspectives as potentially viable and potentially hopeless. But since I am the one tasked with weaving the clues into another tale of the great detective, Soloman Pierce, and not merely recording external reality, I request a little leeway, gentlemen. Detective McPherson makes a valid point. And yet——and yet, what if one single clue prove a talisman? A golden bough the size of a thumbnail? Or a sunglinting stone hinting at the gods?

Treadwell: Nix. You could grow corn at the North Pole with verbiage like that.

Whetstone: But Treadwell, you must understand that a writer relies on more than simple observation. Art is a vital alembic of imagination and memory. Call it, if you will, a hunch.

March Hare: I must remember to write this down. Blast! I ate my pencil.

Treadwell: Hunches have a way of not panning out, Doctor. I once chased a perp through a six block stretch of L.A. real estate that turned out to be a Mack Sennett set. Scared the poor actor half to death.

Soloman: Treadwell is right, Dr. Whetstone. Hunches simply will not do. A detective must always bend his theory around the facts, not the other way around.

March Hare: Exactly. When you have eliminated the impossible, whatever remains, however improbable, must be improbable.

Soloman: Observe a single clue like a scientist observing a single bone. Then trace that bone link by link until you can imagine the full dinosaur. This is the path out of Plato's cave and into the light.

Whetstone: Correct, Holmes, I mean Pierce. And concomitantly, it is my duty as a writer to chart the reader onto a moral course that will enlighten the ignorant.

Treadwell: Sweet Jesus. Hand me that Scotch, Whet.

Soloman: I must apologize, Detective McPherson. The good doctor Whetstone and the rabbit finished off the scotch an hour ago.

Whetstone: Would you like a Cointreau? It was just delivered here this morning by my nursing assistant, Miss Ablution.

(He moves towards the bottle. Treadwell waves him off).

Treadwell: No American male drinks Cointreau. That hinky shit makes you wonder clandestine.

March Hare: The Dormouse must be asleep again. Where is the hot tea? Please answer in the form of a synecdoche.

Treadwell: The point is, Dr. Whetstone, that you have never killed an actual person in your life.

Soloman: Good heavens! Neither have I, Treadwell.

Treadwell: See, that's just my point. Hell, I once shot a princess in the leg! That's the kind of thing that happens when you get your hands dirty in this world. What kind of a murder case is it when the hero doesn't kill people? There's something almost un-American about that. Is that bourbon?

March Hare: Yes it is.

Treadwell: Shoot me a class, will ya?

(The March Hare pours a glass and hands it to Treadwell).

Treadwell: Thank you, Mein Hare. Bottoms up.

March Hare: Oh dear.

Treadwell: What I'm trying to say, gents, is that you got the lineup wrong. The detective doesn't just stand outside the case looking in. The detective IS the case. He's a part of the immediate occasion. No detective, no case, savvy?

Whetstone: But if the detective is the case, then this means...

March Hare: It means that wherever the detective goes, his very presence must *alter* the case.

Treadwell: Afraid so, Bugs.

Whetstone: But this means the case can never be solved!

Treadwell: Well, have you solved the case? No, you just keep following one clue, one bone, after another, until the whole damn planet is one big dinosaur.

March Hare: As the clues get used up?

Treadwell: Exactly.

Whetstone: Then what happens when we run out of clues?

March Hare: Eh-eh—Suppose we change the subject?

Soloman: Stuff and nonsense! There is no mystery that mankind cannot solve. The key is ratiocination. Ratiocination...

Treadwell: And a six shot revolver. Say, this cat's pretty observant for a marsupial.

March Hare: Cat? Where!

Treadwell: Now spill it, Whetstone, which are we? The case, or your story about the case?

Whetstone: If we only knew. Perhaps that is why I always write my cases backwards, like Alice reading the Looking-Glass. Begin with the crime, then work back from there to make sure all the details connect properly.

Soloman: A sound observation, Doctor. All mysteries begin with a death.

Treadwell: And all lives end with one.

Whetstone: True, Mr. Pierce, but one must tread carefully. The stories charting cases of the remarkable Mr. Pierce can do many things, but there is one stricture—They must never give offense.

Treadwell: Never give offense? That's what all my cases do.

Whetstone: Traditional conventions in classical detection must always be observed.

Treadwell: We got some of those "classical conventions" in Hollywood. But they keep creakin', crackin' and fallin' apart.

Soloman: In that case, let us begin with the most important convention of all—the panoptic point of view. Let us begin by composing a composite of our suspect. Doctor Whetson, would you be kind enough to bring me my files on this curious conundrum.

Whetstone (rising and going to a filing cabinet): Of course. How is it filed?

Solomon: Under "Bloody Well Unclear." I did not know how else to title it.

(Whetstone hands him the file and sits. Soloman opens the file with zest).

Now, let us see, let us see…Ah! Here is our suspect! Name: Unknown. Age, height, weight, race, nationality, ambiguous and uncertain. Gender indeterminate. Fingerprints non-existent. Eyewitnesses, possible but strangely silent.

Treadwell: Well we're certainly off to a flying start. By the way, Fluffball, what gender are you?

March Hare: I am a male of course. What else would I be doing here? Female rabbits are pink.

Soloman: Do not despair. Somewhere in this file must lie some clue to our path. The game's afoot!

March Hare: Oh please.

Soloman: Sorry.

Treadwell: Any skinny in there that stays consistent across time?

Soloman: Very little. Our suspect appears to alter appearance with the occasion.

Whetstone: Oh dear lord, not another post-modern poet.

March Hare: Our target appears to be Cheshire Catting us…

Whetstone: And the meaning as well…

Soloman: Indeed. He, she, or it is a master of disguise.

Treadwell: Is he you, chief?

Soloman: Please don't be absurd. I am famous.

Treadwell: Thanks to your friend here.

Soloman: I owe the good doctor a great debt.

Whetstone (feighing modesty, waving his cigar around): Tut-tut. Good writing is simply a matter of skill and precision, of learning to find—what is the word?—Ah! Le Mot Juste!

(He swings his cigar down, accidentally burning the March Hare on the nose).

March Hare: Ahhhhhhhhhhhhhh!

Whetstone: Oh my dear man, I'm so sorry.

March Hare: No worry. Tea will fix it. Tea can fix anything. (He pours himself a cup of tea, adds a healthy dose of bourbon, drinks with satisfaction. He pours some bourbon on his nose). Now, it seems to me that these clues are not leading us anywhere. What is your professional opinion, Treadwell? Please answer in metonymy. Metaphor is passe.

Treadwell: Well it looks like we got us quite a caper. Our culprit appears to be everybody and nobody. What about personal characteristics?

Soloman: Let us look closely: Vindictive. Indifferent. Ruthless. Apathetic. Capable of murdering a million innocent people in one swath, then sparing another murderer or a child. Or taking an entire month just to torture one person to despair.

Whetstone: My God, how do I write this?

Treadwell: Try the bourbon, the writer's guide. Mein Herr seems to like it.

March Hare: It is the tea alone, I assure you.

Treadwell: Let me give it the eyeball.

(Solomon hands him the file. Treadwell reads)

Treadwell: No known address. Hundreds of known aliases. No known motive, but not one victim escapes. Ain't that the definition of victim? The only pattern that remains consistent—the victim ends up on a slab. No explanations forthcoming. We're running in circles here.

(He hands the file back to Soloman, pulls out a pocket notebook).

Whetstone: So you are saying, in other words, that we are like a pack of curs chasing our own tails,

Treadwell: No, Doc, I'm saying the tails are winning. I made a few notes on this putz myself. Listen up. (Reading)

Likes to taunt his pursuers. Drops notes in the street that blow around like Dickensian orphans. Plants false clues to throw off detection. In fact, has planted so many false clues that it has become progressively difficult to distinguish them from real clues, or for that matter, if there are any real clues whatsoever.   Not much to go on, Chief.

Soloman: I do wish you would stop calling me that. It rather puts me out.   Whoever this someone is, they must still be someone. Something happens in history, however we may distort it in our lenses.

Treadwell: History starts and ends with somebody, Soloman. So welcome back to square one. And there's more, just listen: Writes graffiti messages on the walls of London—purporting—to reveal the meaning of life.

Soloman: A specific example, if you will.

Treadwell: Here's one, found scrawled on St. Paul's Cathedral: "Random Boner." Scotland Yard's still trying to decode that one.

Whetstone: Oh dear, I would hate to think that the meaning of life comes down to that.

March Hare: It does in March.

Soloman: Have they identified a handwriting sample?

Treadwell: Nope. Each message turns out to be a forgery of a forgery of a forgery.

Whetstone: No doubt about it, definitely a poet.

Treadwell: The final skinny: This perp is as distinctive as dust and about as much fun as watching other people dance.

Whetstone: Clearly as contemptible a villain as ever to inhabit Whitehall—I mean Whitechapel.

Soloman: Blast this villain, Watson! Give me facts, give me data, give me work! Give me something for my mind to cohere.

March Hare: But all clues are by their nature past tense. The past is an illusion, made of stray bits and pieces, of an image that may or may not have once lay in situ. The future does not exist, since it is mere concept and no more. That only leaves us with the present, which is forever changing under our feet. Hence the tea party goes round and round and round. It's HIM.

Treadwell: Lepus boy has a point. What if we're not all contemporaries? What if we're just a complex of occasions?

Soloman: Can we trace a geneology? If we could identify a father we might be able to trace the son. Or is this another case of pater incertus est?

Whetstone: All this random occasioning in the inscrutable present is pure American. All England is a divine anachronism.

Treadwell: But if the time's off, if it won't behave at all, this means each of us is alone. Which means our little collaboration here is just a fiction itself. (Reads his notebook) Wait. Here's an interesting riff. One of his most recent victims was the famous physicist, Doctor Ray Gamma, author of Everything is Made of Tiny Little Things.

Soloman: What was his theory?

Treadwell: Seems this mug believed our suspect might be supernatural. Glowing in the dark while killing. Like the Hound of the Baskervilles, I guess.

Soloman: Rubbish! A phosphorescent illusion! How did our good doctor pass on?

Treadwell: Apparently he accidentally reversed the X-Ray of Death he'd been working on and sent fifty million rads through his bloodstream. His final word was "Oops!".

Soloman: Most likely this is an example of that most annoying of phenomena—a mere coincidence. Still, this case intrigues. It resembles a mirror-kaleidoscope whose images shift with the slightest change in wind or light.

Whetstone: The very problem I face each time I write. What if the clues are only words after all? What if this case does not even know the words? What if it only hums the melody?

Treadwell: The hum of its own occasion? Well-said, Whetstone. Every crime develops its own momentum as it goes. The criminal always dreams he can keep it under his control, but he can't. No one can. Before long the blood starts to seep out everywhere.

Soloman: So what are we all missing?

(Whetstone and Treadwell stand and face the audience).

Whetstone: Suddenly a wind appeared so fierce and commanding as if to guide the other elements. It was if nature herself were speaking at the window, attempting to tell us why. (He returns to his chair).

Treadwell: That wind really wants in. The wind hates being alone.

(The door opens wide and Fatale Femme enters. She is a beautiful redhead, dressed in a white evening gown that shows off her legs. She wears silk stockings and carries a lit cigarette at the end of a long filter.)

Treadwell: Suddenly the door blows open like wild news and in struts a dame. A dame to make a guy forget he was ever a Boy Scout.

Fatale: Hello boys.

(Whetstone shrieks and covers his eyes. The March Hare plays Blues on a tenor sax.)

Treadwell: Hello, Fatale Femme. Long time no see, dish.

Femme: Hello, Tread. How's tricks? Your dick still private?

Whetstone: Tell me it's not Irene Idler! I cannot abide that woman!

Femme: Whew! What have you gents been smoking? It smells like burnt hair in here.

Treadwell: More than you know. How did it go with my old friend Doctor Ekleberg?

(March Hare pours more tea on his nose).

Femme: Ancient history, McPherson. I just blew into town looking for a little action.

(Soloman stands and bows. Whetstone peers through his fingers).

Soloman: May I offer you a chair?

Whetstone: Great heavens, Holmes, she's beautiful!

(The March Hare tosses his sax, races over and pulls a chair up so Femme can join them. She sits. Soloman sits. The March Hare returns to his chair. Femme takes a long puff of her cigarette and blows it in Whetstone's face. She crosses her legs alluringly. The March Hare's left leg thumps the floor repeatedly. Treadwell returns to his chair, lights another cigarette).

Treadwell: Pierce-Femme, Femme-Pierce. Christ, even that sounds horny.

Femme: A pleasure to meet you, Mr. Soloman Pierce.

Soloman: The pleasure is all mine, Miss—Fatale?

Femme: A pseudonym of course. So many detective novelists kept calling me that so often that the name kind of stuck. But I like it. So I reversed it and threw it on. My real name is Edna. (Shudders)

Whetstone: Do you have any clues to the mystery we are laboring over?

Femme: Not one, Whet. It's all a mystery to me. Not that I'm an amateur when it comes to sleuthing around. Let's take you, Mr. Pierce.

Soloman: Yes? Me?

Femme: I see you are wearing your favorite smoking jacket, the same as in Mr. Whetstone's stories, and that you have worn it all night, since it is wrinkled, and furthermore, the indentations and pipe ash suggest recent use. All this suggests you have been pursuing a particularly difficult and complex case, even for your famous detective skills. Your pupils are bloodshot, which is supporting evidence, though they also show signs of recent cocaine use.

Soloman: Remarkable, Miss Fatale! Your observation skills are quite impressive.

Femme: Here to help. Nobody knows the deceptive mind better than I. I've been around men all my life.

March Hare: I have a modest question, Miss Femme. Would you ever consider mating outside your species? Please answer in the form of a syllogism.

Femme: Not just yet, Thumper. Although, specifically: All men are beasts. Soloman is a man. Therefore, Soloman is…

Soloman: Might you allow me a cross-examination?

Femme: Have at it, ace.

Soloman (Nervously): Let me see. I…I…

Femme: Yes?

Soloman: Ah! Based on details the average mortal overlooks, I would say you are female. A—Attractive. Hair: Red. Mouth: Red. Eyes: Tempting I mean tinted with green flecks. A smoker. You prefer your cigarettes filtered. You move oddly when you walk, especially in your lower portions, favor silk stockings, cross your legs, and (Voice goes way high)—enjoy vigorous sex with manly men.

Whetstone: Amazing as always, Mr. Soloman Pierce! I am left breathless.

Femme: As I've said to too many men—close but not quite. Look, I've been used by writers and other defectives for years to supply easy solutions to cases they can't solve. Whenever there's a culprit to be found, and the dimwit is too flummoxed for a clean solve, he drags me back into the story.

Soloman (embarrassed): Meaning no offense, Miss Femme, but we are exploring a rather difficult case.

Femme: What case? You don't have any case and you know it. Haven't you read the newspapers? You can't locate the criminal when crime's gone incorporated.

Treadwell: Face it, she's right. All human history's just a roll of the dice.

Femme: Or a roll in the hay?

Whetstone: I'm sorry but I object to this line of thought. You are overlooking the key metaphysical aspect of the perfectly-crafted detective tale.

Femme (to Treadwell): What the fun is "metaphysical"?

Treadwell: It's the philosophical equivalent of a one-size-fits-all condom.

Femme: Tut-tut, Tread. Now listen up, boys. I can supply you with one vital link in your dinosaur.

Soloman: Which is? Is it a vital clue?

Femme: There are no vital clues. There's only a total situation. But I can guarantee you your culprit is a male.

Soloman: But how do you know this? Did you arrive at your conclusion through careful inductive reasoning?

Femme: Nah. That's the hooey. It's simple. Right in front of you. A purloined letter.

Whetstone: We have covered all those forged letters.

Femme: Not a literal letter, Whethead. It's a question, not an answer: Who else but a man could ever kill this way? Who else but a man would make murder an art form?

 Whetstone: No no. I know my craft.

Femme: Face it. Men invented death. Women invented life.

(She stands. Men and rabbit stand with her).

Treadwell: Hear-hear. Want to grab a drink, Femme? For old time's sake?

Femme: Not now, sweet. I came to take London for a stroll.

(Fatale and Treadwell face the audience, taking the same positions that Treadwell and Whetstone took as the play opened).

Soloman: But—but what about evil? (He sits. Whetstone and the March Hare sit).

Treadwell: I don't know, that's one case I've never solved. All I know, brother, is this: Life ain't no catechism. It's more like that night you've gone to the same bar night after night searching for the big solution, and you're lost, you know you are, so damn alone your bones feel like singing it, and then one night—(He looks over at Femme)...You see a vision, a real knockout, and you know right then the clues have all been tossed away, and she lowers this mask and she's all goddess and you're hooked for good and your bones start to sing a different tune, and for now, for now, everything seems solved or at least feels that way. Coincidence or fate, that one encounter has changed your whole life. That's the only real mystery worth solving.

Femme: Good night, gentleman.

Soloman (Standing): Please—won't you—stay? (He sits).

Femme: Sorry, Soloman. I've got a world to rattle, out there somewhere in the wind. Out there somewhere in the wind and fog even now beautiful girls are dying in lieu of angels, and somewhere in Ohio, other beautiful girls are sitting on their front porch swings hoping to plot their hearts through the mystery.

(She exits. Treadwell slowly returns to his seat, pours himself a drink. As the play closes, the lights grow dimmer and dimmer until at the end the stage is in pure darkness).

Treadwell: What a dame! Well, what is that beautiful mind of yours thinking now, Pierce?

Soloman: I'm thinking. I'm remembering the time I saw *Hamlet* at the Old Vic. A most enlightening experience. The actor playing Hamlet, after so many performances and God knows how many rehearsals, was clearly becoming angry and frustrated with his role. I could almost hear him thinking: What the bloody hell is really going on in this damn unactable play? So he left. He just walked off the stage and took a seat in the audience next to me. Maybe he thought it could help—I don't know.

Perhaps he felt that if he could step outside the play and survey the stage as a whole, he could uncover some clue as to the author's intention. But when we looked up, the entire cast—the whole court at Elsinore— stood frozen in their places. It was if they were thinking, What the bloody hell does he think he's doing? There can be no *Hamlet* without Hamlet. And when I looked over at the actor, he was crying.

Treadwell: Gentlemen, I think I know where the clue lies that will solve all our problems.

Soloman: Where?

Treadwell: No-Man's-Land.

(Curtain)

Part Two: Youth

Memory snake

Our father
waters us,
grows us
in the long green garden
into the way of the fathers,
his coiled-snake hose in his hands.
My brother and I
run and leap and dodge
his missiles,
his machine-gun sprays,
his laughter flooding the light.
There is no escape.
Richochets hiss the rose's huge
kisswound
as our flesh turns white to red
and we fall, drop by drop, through time,
and something watches in the waiting dark
as all the weeds cry thirsting for the stars.

Rock of secrets

Age five, I found a common-looking rock
that broke open in my hands
like an overdone potato
to reveal an inner world,
a jeweled kaleidoscope
thirsting for light.
Flecks of mica black as fisheyes
longing for the dark side of the moon,
quartz embedded
like a memory inside a dream,
crystals clenched in strength of years
like clues to an unnamed mystery.
It seemed to recognize me
as though I were the one lost
for centuries, abandoned to the lonely
fate of alley stones and castaway stars,
though I think I knew even then,
it belonged to another world.
So I left it for someone else to find
in my secret field where
gods and monsters hid.
And from that day I have never
seen rocks or stones or trees
or people, the same way.

The forever wound

I was the player,
I was the one
who moved the eternal battles,
indoors or out.
I had no idea
why we were all fighting.
I only knew
the Blue were supposed to win,
had more men and cannons.
I hated the dead Grey one.
For heaven's sake get up!
There are medals, songs, and glory,
and all the pretty girls will love you
forever and ever.
But the worst was the wounded Blue one,
gasping forever in silence, forever
falling, gun tripping on nothing,
never fallen, never dead, never a hero,
his mouth propped in wordless pain.
Clutching his plastic heart,
eyes blank with mystery,
wide open without a why.
That one came in nightmares.
That one was forever my own.

A dead soldier speaks

My death came cupped in a shell
no larger than a hazelnut,
and yet it sent my world to darkness,
and showed me the depths of silence.
You who claim to speak for the dead
speak nothing, your lies like a magician
pulling silk scarves from his mouth.
Death is the last bow of the magician.
How do you know I blessed my mother's name,
praised God or country, or was grateful
it was I and not another? I would rather
my killer speak these lines than you.
My death was even smaller than my life.
The shot cut my voice away from why.
The end was sudden and complete.
My bones went merely stepping down.
We are buried beneath the reasons,
tongue-less, eyeless, hearts exterminated.
Beyond all dreams of redemption,
the leaves wind questions round our graves.

The Witness I

My first murder
was a Hollywood stunt man,
an untermensch of dreams,
extra-deep in the death-blue cavalry,
who caught a Cheyenne arrow
straight through his eye,
and died with no medal or why.
I-saw-it. Jesus—
Was I the only witness?
Yes. Everyone else was watching the Duke
prance another victory of lead
over the evil unscrupulous reds.
That nameless Private taught me difference
in his short lonely life of yikes—
who wins, who loses, who gets
the girl and the new sheriff's badge,
and who gets pitched without glory
into dusty re-runs of history.
I was there. I saw. I did not suffer,
sharing my popcorn with Frankenstein,
who always yelled "Good! Good!"
whenever another pointless peasant
got pitched from a convenient cliff.
But he raged at his exile in the rain,
and wept each time the torches came.
By the time I turned pure zombie,
I reckon I'd seen a thousand murders,
several hundred strangulations,
countless shootings and stabbings,

ever more inventive ways to die,
and one lone arrow, straight through the eye.
So you see—
Dahmer and Gacy have nothing on me.
And January 6th? A Sunday matinee.

The First Hero

I'll tell you how it happened.
Three cave men—Nero, Slug, and Arnold
were trapped on a dizzy high ledge
by a saber-tooth tiger
whose vision was pure hunger.
Nero and Slug improvised a philosophy:
"The Weakest Goes." So they tossed Arnold.
He tumbled east to west to north to south
into the waiting mouth of that grateful cat.
The two survivors laughed and celebrated.
But when they returned, all the villagers asked:
"Where's old Arnold?" Nero and Slug wept.
"He bravely sacrificed himself for us!"
The stunned villagers built a statue of Arnold,
then a temple, with a motto: "He died so we could evolve."
But Arnold did not die. He curled clenched
inside that tiger like a rare and strange gestation.
Through tiger eyes inscrutable he saw
the world striped and lush and vibrant
with secrets, hunger the seed of all leapings.
He read on the shore's dark scroll
all the fables of the drowned.
Beneath the caparison of jewels and jungle
he surveyed his ancient inheritance
while the stars shivered in joyful loneliness.
Nero and Slug died, spread low among the fossils.
But Arnold, who invented statues, temples,
heroes and mourning, all with one tumble,
lives on, and in his padding paws he feels
the power that once made gods suffice.

Dance with dark and light

(for Tom Beery)

And I'm leaping from streetlight to streetlight
like an electron evading certainty,
cones of light embracing me gold and neon,
skeleton fire escapes releasing shadows
that felon-creep behind me street to street.
Safe! The Phantom, unmasked, disguises him-
self as silence. Shhh! Demons drink up the bars.
Dracula hangs upside-down from Pluto and
I run as Godzilla brushes the stars green and glowing,
and zombies come shopping for heads.
The fear crouches with me between the lights,
feeding itself on shadows and I am become
death and fearless joy while stoplights
cast their jewels to eternity, and all of this
is my own private theater of doom.
All I touch burns with irradiated
possibility, and it's alive and I'm
alive, and the peasants with their torches
weaving questions through the night and I
alone cast this night to visions.
I wait in the light for now, for now,
till my next crazy leap through the dark.
I won't leave till my whole heart is haunted,
and there are at least a thousand ways to die.
Such a paradise of monsters!

From The Secret Diary of Lucy Westenra

The little liar got it all wrong.
The bed of fertile earth was mine to grow,
as he lay in his lair, and Lord Arthur,
the fool, dreamed of my pure inanities.
A lord, a doctor, a cowboy, a count,
each thought he alone could rule me.
I played them like the peasants they were,
the last with a hole in his empty heart.
Now I lie back in my silken nightgown
and wait for darkness to tempt the moon,
my breaths rising and falling with the wind,
the crucifix tucked beneath my pillow.
Now comes the storm to spread wide my casements.
Now come green waters to sing in my ears.
I rise, float free, ascend to divine lust,
I the master of my darkest dreams.

House of Dreams and Demons

That house left us messages
I found behind the wallpaper.
They did not approve of our designs.
My father, my brother and I,
our nails, hammers and levels,
our dreams of order in place.
Our heartless hammers crucified
those walls, floors, ceilings—
trying to pound them into sense.
No good. The house resisted us.
Levels unleveled, boards snapped, and
shadows crouched in corners waiting.
Plaster fell, aging my father's hair.
His curses flew around the roof
like bats searching for a haunt.
No, no, I can't go back there—
where ghosts stuttered from my bed
where my uncle died before the sirens.
One cold finger pointed at the wall
as if in accusation, or to say it's here,
the thing you long and fear to know.
That was long ago and yesterday,
present and gone like trapped bird wings
beating their blood into glass.
I survived by hiding in the blue-green
visions painted on the living room floor
by my mother's stained-glass windows.
They knew, they dreamed and hung on,
like the graceful wings of a dragonfly
pulsing in sunrise.

The Girdle

Mrs. Brownstone, widow, came equipped
with a girdle, swish, beehive hairdo,
pink lipstick, and pinch-tight high-heeled shoes
that made her walk like a Disney toy.
Audrey Hepburn gloves, silk stockings,
a set of fresh teeth, the neighbors whispered,
and mascara of midnight blue.
She was ready for action.
That girdle I could see
right through her every dress,
clenching tight a passionate embrace,
though she was hardly overweight.
I watched her through my bedroom window,
the parties she flung that dared the night in,
her cigarette tipped on a magician's cane
like a floating exclamation point.
The neighbors surrounded her house with eyes,
peering and piercing for secrets.
I studied Sears Roebuck ladies' underwear,
those inviting and forbidding angels.
I followed her with my dad's binoculars
as she squeaked and clicked down the sidewalks
to whisper secrets to the mannequins on Main.
Rumors followed and circled her like bees.
When her house burned down the bees tsked-tsked.
Some hummed she was knock-down-drunk.
Others buzzed of a rejected lover's rage.
I like to think she burned it down herself.
Leaving behind in the thoughtless ashes,

her magic wand, a pair of high-heeled shoes,
two slender, white, long silk gloves,
and a girdle her discarded halo.

Summer of '62

Where were you when I was nowhere
sane, dreaming irradiated rain in my forever
lostness dark and longing whispering walls,
silence the only language I knew?
Dream your way back to the real whatever,
that hula-hoop apocalypse, rainbowed gravity,
erector-set of stars, climbing to fission,
Martian cancer burning in our blood
You remember? The little girl
whose heart was burned, her brother
whose arms were found in the trees?
So it's Summer '62. Tupperware skies.
The dishwasher whispers to the H-Bomb.
our hearts quivering in corners with the spiders,
imagination a player piano with all white
keys, a dance for the uninvited, sweeping
ghosts like cobwebs into the bomb shelter.
Houses line themselves in Dewey Decimals,
each different in exactly the same way,
each with its own cul-de-sac ouroboros,
their nervous antennae sweeping the skies
for enemies, outside or within, an
inner ear of highways, closed system.
All we want is a good night's sleep, but
we know the whole blind universe
could collapse like a pocket telescope
if the Cheshire Cat sneezes, or if the
Red King awakens from his dream.
A shaking. Is it thunder? We pray that it is

thunder. There's a message clicking from
the stars. It shivers the multi-colored suckers
strung from the ceiling at Woolworth's
It frightens the old men in the odd, bent
alleys behind the American dream.

It passes from mailman to mailman
to paperboy, who slides it beneath
your door, or hides it inside the newspaper
that unfolds all your fears. Mayor announces
fair weather unless…ignore the purple cloud…duck
and cover, lonely hearts, the children, glowing with…
ate the bark from the trees, hunting sale…dis-
count…your soul?…invite your friends and family.
The envelope with the secret answer
must not be opened at any cost.
People have disappeared for asking why.
Answers have disappeared in lieu of questions.
All the air speaks rockets, rockets, rockets…to empty
the sky of angels, as X-15's crucify the sky.
And when they cart the bodies away,
we pretend there's no message for real,
nothing for keeps. Fiction is fiction
after all.

The candy apocalypse

Imagine an entire civilization
edging on annihilation, pushed
there by a little red candy ball,
but it did we did we sucked
"Atomic Fireballs" red to white
like child vampires so don't tell
me someone didn't want us
cringing in our tears brooding
death could come any day any
night any how without a why
any second Mrs. Dornberger
might creep to our third grade
window release her antennae
through the top of her head narrow
her already narrow eyes peer at
the horizon and scream "Here come
the Russian planes!" and we all had
to duck and cover under our desks
a whole nation of turtles polishing
our shells oh hell with that I
would hide inside my locker hoping
it was lined with healthy lead besides
through the slots I could watch Mrs.
Dornberger burn down to a cigar stub
but the Black kids still could not drink
from our drinking fountain even on their
death day but it looked like a urinal any-
way just like the back alleys of our
hometown where the homeless dragged

themselves like bent discarded cigarettes
they couldn't afford our Atomic Fireballs
and neither could we which is probably why
we stole ours and stuffed them overflowing
from our desks and one day Fritz my beagle
followed me to school unseen by me slipped
through the emergency exit and peered into
our classroom with a look that said: "What—
you're all not dead yet?" But in a way we

were all dead already afraid to live or even
breathe too loud dead as warmed-over toast
or Zwieback eaten straight from the box I
was dead certain some evil Whosit from the
planet Yikes wanted us all terrorized crawling for
air while the whole damn stratosphere lit up
like Christmas in Hell with X-15's scrawling a
desperate message in the sky and sirens, sirens,
sirens, and Zontar releasing bats from his balls to
control our minds but wait I was talking about
Atomic Fireballs and how they ruled our hearts
and minds Jesus even our favorite candy glowed
in the dark and ate us alive inside-to-out and Fat
Raymond held the record he sucked down eight
fireballs at once but we hated Fat Raymond more
on that later and anyway I was the greater fool since
I was stupidly convinced that if I could just swallow
enough of those sugar-coated cherry bombs I
would grow to glow irradiated power like God-
zilla banging his tail on Tokyo clicking his claws
and glowing beyond extinction I'd stick it to all
the adults who scared me eternal and kept me
forever hiding with my clutches of Atomic Fireballs
I'd line my desk with them to repel the firestorm

as it sucked the air from Mrs. Dornberger's baggy
lungs how I'd laugh that day as she clutched her
bony chest and gulped in pure plutonium till her
eyes bugged out and exploded I was only helping
her learn to see what we saw every day and night
especially night in our dreams where we clawed
and clawed and dug through earth searching for
the North Pole to cool our charred skin with the
melting polar ice cap all kids of all colors finally
slaking their thirst while the teens danced to the
Von Braun Blues trauma in the burning libraries
of the sun and even that was just an everyday
apocalypse you got used to them after all while
like you got used to men in yellow raincoats
waiting outside the school to offer you candy
in their cars and talcum powder cigarettes that

sucked you into your gagging future and blasting
caps that dropped in devilish glee from the
backs of bouncing construction zone trucks and
lay there looking like an innocent toy whistle but
if you picked one up from the ground and blew
through it it would blow your fucking head off
there was even a tv commercial of a cartoon kid
picking one up to merely whistle and getting
boomed into eternal silence and invisibility
that would be fun I thought, pure invisibility
what a gas what a nice way out of it that terror
of forever being seen being a target of some
lunatic with a cause now do you see why we
consumed Atomic Fireballs like there was no
tomorrow they were our only defense it was
like taking all the fear and horror inside your-

self and learning to live with it to just get along
we devoured them Eucharist wafers like sal-
vation like an eternal recess I even developed
a strong enough immunity that sometimes I
would crunch one in one bite just to get the
full effect of simulating my head exploding
that's how I staved off my fear of those
blasting caps lying in wait for me on every
street corner gnawing and gnawing on their
peppery pow as we watched 3-D monsters
with glandular conditions they got from feeding
on Los Alamos until they grew like they were
eating their Wonder Bread daily and could get
back at the adults we hated by chasing them
through entire cities and the adults who did not
know our atomic secrets were so blind to horror
that they always ran in the same direction the
monster was coming and got eaten or smothered
or crushed or burned to cinders as the big beastie
left his slimy trail through downtown Metropolis
as we laughed and pointed and mocked and feasted
on death and popcorn the only time we weren't as
afraid as cringing spiders sensing the coming flames
oh hell we were the children of doom and Kool-Aid
chased by giant ants and mutants as we tossed

Atomic Fireballs at them as they chased us down
the stairs to the CD air-raid shelter which for some
reason some idiot built beneath the museum with
its creeping silences and its diorama of the Shawnee
chief stuffed and poised for eternity forever being
shot to death by our town founder with a gun shaped
like a cornucopia while Fat Raymond could never

keep up with us to hell with him anyway we hated
Fat Raymond his parents ignored him which we envied
but they gave him everything we could never afford like
baseball cards comic books toys cap guns air bazookas
whole armies of plastic soldiers we'd steal from him and
melt into goo in his family's charcoal grill that reminded us
of our future and over a dozen G.I. Joes training us all for
Vietnam so why should we not hate him hell even butterflies
hated him they'd spot him pumping his big ten speed groaning
under the enormous bulk of him gasping for air red cheeks bulging
so he looked like a giant Atomic Fireball coming to explode on us
but luckily butterflies despised him they'd chase him down the sidewalk
on his bike as he flailed at them with his pink pudgy palms crammed
with Atomic Fireballs so we locked him out of the bomb shelter and
left him out there to face the butterflies and block-busters and laughed
while he pounded and screamed at the security door what the hell
it was only a small tornado nosing its way down Main Street not what
we'd first thought besides compared to us he had it easy we were
stuck in this hellhole with a moldy toilet, a survival guide missing
its last page, packets of dried eggs a broken flashlight and a fire
extinguisher what kind of air raid shelter needs a fire extinguisher
but after a while his screams got annoying so as we heard his
enormous weight breaking through the safety door we left by the
fire escape that stepped up to Mars as the stars held their breath
in horror as the moon hanged herself just to see what it might
be like though Fat Raymond tracked us by following the trail of
Atomic Fireballs we dropped as we ran and cursed that the
world was still here
after all but nobody cared that was the same cornball ending to
every monster and alien-invasion film we ever saw so we weren't
buying any of it we had reached the point where we were fine with
self-annihilation anyway who cares just get it over with, you
Hollywood

world of fakery just blow us all to kingdom come hell I'd
volunteer to

ride the final Atomic Fireball myself right down onto this joke
humanity because we alone were the survivors and each time we
imagined another apocalypse we were free, free for now until
tonight's nightmares would teach us again how to dream true.

The cat from Hiroshima

There was a cat from Hiroshima
who glowed gold like the lusts of men.
You tossed him out each night,
kicked him, denied him, pretended
he never was, but he always returned,
loyal to you, caressing you
with his radiant purr.
Now daylight is delirium,
now hallucination has eyes,
now the cat's eyes contain your own.
The cat won't let you rise,
breathes in your every prayer
and laps up all your fears.
Now the sky dreams its own destruction,
and the cat is on the prowl, howling
for the shadows blown to the walls
of the school ground where the ghosts
of children dance and dance and dance…

Playing fake baseball for keeps

Closing day the sky a carnival mirror,
my baseball machine where it's always June,
though it now bleeds tears of rust,
and the crowd here never laughs, moves or cries.
It's nineteen sixty-three
months till Kennedy's brains blow roses
in poisoned Dallas wind, and America
is cute, dumb and happy as a steaming
wet hot dog though behind the
funhouse, itinerant Mexican workers
watch the lights from the railroad tracks.
The ancient machine stutters out a steel
ball, I flick my flippers and score a double!
A tin Babe Ruth glides, sticks, takes his base.
(A home run will light up your own
private apocalypse).
Still, I'm afraid of what I'll find when the
lights die out. Half my All-Star team is
dead and buried, the crowd a painted lie.
But my pockets sag with unearned nickels.
So if I play each pitch just right,
I might just last forever.

Coal cellar

Mr. Steaman fed his house
coal, his gold tomcat perched
on top of the heap, eyes like
twin hovering moons, and when
the coal ran low, he pitched in
random boards he found in alleys,
cardboard boxes, shoved in entire
treetops, the small trees that sprout
in vacant Midwestern lots and grow
like hunger, and the coal burned
ice blue to meteor gold and red, and
the treetops burst into suns.
But it was never enough
to feed that exhausted, hungry
house, whose floorboards bent like
pirate planks, whose windows, blinded
with ash, barely saw the world, and
Mrs. Steaman's eyes seemed as lost
as celestial birds.
He shoveled in fears, and hopes, and
dreams and despair, and all his kids
grew like outrageous weeds in Summer, though
Fall was his time of year, season of burning
endings to begin again, since Mr. Steaman
knew everything is burning—stars and sun
and earth and flesh and time—whole universes
alive with fire. And black tongues speaking
chimney to chimney.

Alive in the death cult

Shop class, 1971—
you can make an ash tray
or a wooden cat.
I make a wooden cat
that looks like an ash tray.
My friend Todd Rush
made a bomb.
He should have made an ash tray
to sweep himself up
after he was exploded in Vietnam.
But today is our annual
Don't-Get-Shot-Or-Stabbed Day
at Lima Senior High, replete with
future Klansmen, Black Panthers,
and warriors for peace and love.
We are the children of blood and hate,
from Dealey Plaza to Kent State,
all our heroes
shot or suicided. Only America
catastrophizes itself.
It's a shame about Miss Ray,
whose fiancé went M.I.A.
way over there. One day
she just started screaming at the walls,
then disappeared in moonlight.
Perhaps I am already dead
here and now, inside this skin,
and simply don't know it, breathing
counterfeit air. Death
has a gift for surprises.

36

Thomas Null, machine 36, the hole-puncher,
was secretly apprenticed to despair.
I thought he was wise, since he laughed at silence.
Then one day he disappeared mid-shift,
and I found him dead on his front porch swing.
It was only when I walked his route alone
that I saw the cruel genius of his escape.
Saints & Sinners, No Answer, The Alibi,
Utopia—a bar on every corner.
He must have seen he could drink his way home.
His eyes had captured something of the sky,
lonely angels still clinging to the wind.

Journeys are ways of marking out a distance

"Journeys are ways of marking out a distance,
Or dealing with the past, however ineffectually,
Or ways of searching some new enclosure in this space
Between the oceans…"
                                             —Weldon Keys,

"Travels in North America"

                    I
As if time had hidden recesses
where the silence lives…
Brother you've left me here,
returned to where I cannot find you.
But if somehow we could go back?
Before Autumn winds taught us distance,
though such a task seems similar
to guessing the next leaf's fall
All words seek an origin,
that purity of first breath-cry,
yet words get sidetracked like random toys,
and memories rearrange the furniture.
Grey hairs dream only of the past
Old age comes on like an illness,
and an illness can only go
one way or the other.
I know the perils of return,
the voice, distant yet dangerously close,
creeping down the coiled cord and
strangering the voice on the phone.

"Tell your father
he's a dirty nigger-lover,
and we know
where you walk to school."

Brother, why do you walk forever
ahead of me? I watch you turn
and speak but I can't hear you,
my own voice too enmeshed in time.
We both thought you could never die,
yet your face seems here and far away,
like the shadow of a frightened bird,
held for just one moment in the grass.

II

"The past is yours, to keep invisible if you wish
but also to make absurd evaluations with
and in this way prolong your dream of non-discovery."
            —John Ashbery, "Clepsydra"

The Black kids were kept in the balcony,
where their dreams hovered over light
while Alan Ladd gunned Jack Wilson
and lost his chance for love.
Brother you pounded a hole
clean through the living room wall
though I never learned why, some
misery you hid from us all.
I ran and hid in the Sigma Theater
where Tarzan drowned an African king.
I would sneak into the balcony
to stare in wonder at the chandelier

Waiting and longing for the Phantom,
clenching his saw of justice and revenge
Come, ghost, cut the chains free,
and crash my dreams to visions!

III

Yet to return and find the hidden purity
I thought I heard between your sighs.
My magic alley—to remember the emotions
there, the hum of colors, and their echoes.
Wet stones that glittered meanings
in the sun. Like keys to
a secret kingdom, while towering
weeds taught patience to the winds.
Somehow I was always going to heaven,
and though I never arrived, I learned to
feel the long grasses in my breath and blood,
teaching me the green within the green.
Brother by day the stained glass panes
shown down on the living room floor
as if angels, bored with white radiance,
had cast their lot with our world.
At night we wove the air with whispers,
yet our love needed only silence, in our
beds, late at night, the leaning trees
sighed outside our windows, guarding our dreams.
One day you built a castle of snow,
lined it with menacing skulls.
"We can hide in here," you said. You knew something.
But those skulls said keep out, keep out, keep out.
In the grey distance the courthouse clock
—still unfinished—pointed nowhere—

just numbers circling forever, and
bell chimes empty of time.

One day your fort was empty.
None of my cries availed. Brother, why
did you leave me?
Where have you gone in the Winter winds?

IV

Now I have returned
in a dream
to reclaim my long-lost kingdom,
castle-courthouse-theater—home.
Yet they seem mere clever replicas.
The snow falls like confetti. I am not
a child in this dream but a man, dropped
into the past to see it again.
I try to focus, but the light refuses
to cooperate, will not sparkle or
glint of fields of angels. Things
just are, in their blank refusal.
I place my hand on a wall of our house,
and the whole house shakes like a set prop,
while outside the bedroom window, the trees
seem painted and pained with fear.
The Sigma Theater is composed
entirely of juxtaposed images.
Only the balcony is real, and from it
comes a chorus of cries and weeping.

V

I see myself now as a child,
watching my life on the movie screen.
I cannot change or stop it. The cone of
light seems a captured angel.
Miss Blanc divides our first grade class in two.
"Mr. Kennedy wants the white
children and the niggers all together.
But God made us to be separate."
Now I see: it was always double. The fall
was far behind us, brother my love.
The pain's felt fully only later, will not leave,
for now it has finally found a home.
I watch my child-self chased down my alley
by three bullies with popsicle stick knives.
I had forgotten this, and now can't change it,
this happening that has happened before.
I see myself clutching a pure black gumball—
rare—a gift of a rare fate's penny—
The alley glitters its icicle teeth.
it will not bless or help.
I watch myself fall and the black ball sinks
down and down a puddle mirroring blue.
I long to follow it to my lost world,
deep in my alleyway of dreams.
But I am now a child inside a man, brother,
outside the walls of your lonely snow castle.
You are gone forever, and remembering
is like stepping through holes in the wind.
A train rolls by, goes who knew, who knew, who knew…
Time is now some ancient land—far, far to the north.
Strange how love remains forever,
coursing our blood with memory.

Part Three: Age

The Giant Pyrfera

They are returning again,
these forever falling and fallen,
raining from the high blue light.
My roots remain. Theirs are all severed.
Some writhe and kick. Why?
There is no return from down here.
Strange how they only bloom into bones,
while I guard their treasure of suns.
Their red comes trailing after,
ribboning like eels.
My green stays unstained and pure.
I can feel it drink the light.
Look how they have lost their third arms,
pointed and gleaming as shark's teeth.
Their jellyfish eyes stare at nothing,
then fill with stars and moons.
Finally, their many-armed mother,
groaning, moaning, mourning her lost children,
twists and spirals down the great Memory
to here, my garden of peace.

Night-driving

Night-driving, at times,
is pure blind negotiation,
a dance of random curves,
rain soaking up the light,
lines pointing somewhere or nowhere.
I advised my son to follow his dreams
and he did—all the way to a university
hundreds of miles away and now I return,
as we all must return, over and again,
to silence waiting in empty rooms.
The father says go, and be, and grow.
The child in the man says stay, please stay.
I feel like the one piano key that sticks,
and now barely remembers the song
whose melody seemed all the world.
My mind and clutch are coming apart.
Both are known to grate and rattle.
Sometimes hell is just returning.
I pray, when I finally arrive, memory
waits up for me, leaving the porch light on.

Atropos on Main

The clock seems nervous on the wall.
The barber's scissors glitter and snip,
a silver shark searching round my scalp.
Three men wait, hands on knees.
One sleeps, his face like
the hollows of a palm.
Here comes the electric razor,
invisible hornet, homing,
pierces the thin-spun silence.
My hairs tumble in clumps,
like mown-down Confederate soldiers,
remnants of lies and lost causes.
Now the final scissors near—
all the faces I've ever loved
mirrored in its patient blades.
As I exit, the barber sweeps
various heads into a bag.
The clock hand jerks—three o'clock.

The white van

It's back again.
The white van, it seems only I can see.
One day they'll say:
There's no more Sean!
One exclamation point,
fade to mere period,
then just blank white space.
This morning it's circling the block,
like it's out selling Death Ice Cream.
Mother of beauty, it got old Mr. Whosit!
I just have to look—two shameless feet
poking from a sheet in the sun.
I see people going on their way.
They do not seem to see a thing.
Now it's down by Mrs. Whatshername's.
Is there a pattern—no, it must be random.
Now it's nosing down the back alley.
When it does come for me, I don't want to come back
as a tree, river, mountain or wave.
These simply will not suffice.
All I need is hundred more lives
to finally get one right.

Dispossessions

Joso:
"Colder even than snow,
the Winter moon
on white hairs"
is how time must travel,
appalling the body
mind and blood
and misplacing words
once safe at home.
Even home now a mystery,
leaving us clues to the gone.
My father's glasses
found in an old drawer,
known first by my hand.
How will he see in the other world?
Or read words he left behind?
A gnawed old pen—
even our teeth marks
survive us.
His suits hang alone,
keeping his Rexall After-Shave
scent.
The past is empty but
to touch, scent, or sounds
between silences.
My mother's song
still haunting
her swing.
A fence in a snowfield

divides nothing from itself.
We inherit
only the blank page,
a sliver of the moon.

Insomnia caravan

Dark, pure dark
is where thinking breeds
and falls apart since light
only displaces the night and
stars are wounded in time
as the deep wilderness
presses out its beasts.
This insomniac moon
refuses to set, two a.m.,
nowhere hour, the odd, bent
hour that never seems to know
what it wants or where it wants
to go. I try to speak to it, but
my words hide in their secret worlds.
Man simply is, says Sartre,
at least until he is not. Then
what?   The darkness may be dreams
or demons or diamonds. It might be diamonds.
Like the lovely girls I knew so long ago, who
were taught never to sing their hearts.
I know I'm alone and must enter the earth.
But which I would that be?
We need pinpoints, bulletin boards, timetables,
but death is notoriously casual.
I need the eight-legged patience of a garden
spider, clenched in the shade, or weaving its
spontaneous bop prosody through the skies.
Conspiracy of moon and shadows—
I only know I'm with the Roma—always—

forever trailing the margins of exile, the moon's
exile, and our own, their caravan moving out
again, beaten from their lands, so are we
all Roma, beneath the calix of stars,
searching for a home beyond these wounds.

Tower in Winter Woods

It is an ancient wood
that's dreaming me on and on,
and the dream guides me
where I know I must go
again and again
where the bare trees grow
from the lowering skies,
arterial, veined in black,
here where my private tower
awaits me in silent menace.
My crow perches, clutched to a thorn,
a question mark in the endless white.
Here where light devours itself. I only know
this time the fox and owl have moved in for good.
And only the crow knows where this will end.
All I know—I return willingly, even if
my wounds decorate the sky, to meet these
three secret messengers, my animal spirits
who have known me since before time,
and know full well what I must do.
And I promise them to return again,
forever, if need be,
until I turn this barren place to Spring,
until I finally learn
to sleep on a blade of grass.

Dead Guy on a Horse

Statues make annoying travel companions.
They never laugh, cry, giggle, sneeze,
burp, fart, make love, throw up, give up,
start over, surrender, show joy or compassion.
Worst of all, they never show regret.
Not for anything: Murder, death, war, blood,
sacrifice of children. There is something inhuman
about a man with no regrets.
So rope this old bastard down.
He's not art, he's taxidermy.
I distrust his sword, aimed at the heart of God.
I distrust his cold eyes of stone.
Stuff him in a museum,
where silence is holier than sermons,
where children can study how not to live their lives,
and the past can be seen eye to eye.

On the day of another American mass-shooting

The way of the Fathers has become the way of death,
from Mystic, Connecticut to Uvalde Texas.
We must abandon this trail of horrors.
The daylight burns like psychotherapy.
The night cools and soothes nothing.
Spring no longer speaks to us.
Death is now a national holiday,
violence our religion, our flags
forever strung at half-mast.
Evil adheres in the syntax of madmen
who believe that blood redeems the violent.
Thoughts and prayers—useless as silence.

The ant poets

Ants are poets...
careful, determined, patient
construction workers.
In my brick driveway
they assemble their gunpowder hills,
with a tiny hole in the top,
like there's a spirit breathing down there.
Is it memory?
Because when the inevitable
storm arrives, washes away
their kingdom of dreams,
the next day the castle has returned.
They are the original escape-pests.
They survive.
They are down there now
waiting, clenched in darkness,
plotting their return to light.
Poets need umbrellas
to unfold their doom predictions.
But I'd rather drown in every random storm
if I could build like these.

The end of nightmares

I dreamed that Man died but the animals lived.
Mourning doves watching the lamps go blind,
coyotes yawning in the hearts of machines,
sparrows thrilling in the eaves.
Perfection of insects in grass free of "green,"
beetles swagger over our unlined graves.
Dragonflies thread stars with filament wings,
as mantis shadows unfold the darkness.
The horse's mane waves the riderless winds.
The leopard's uncaptured, shining lust
reclaims her Asia, and the rabbit's blood
floods the fox's teeth with ecstasy.
Breathless spirit of hunger, hunt, and wound,
holy thirst, delights of flight and fear,
and raptured by the cobra's diamond gaze,
the night bird sings no other world.
They sleep in the easeful dust of kings,
dreaming beneath empty, eastern skies,
breeding, dying, born and reborn, they
awake to their own startled cries.
No humans, devils or angels remain,
not a war, not a suicide, not one rape
or crucifixion, only the animals, living
for the divinity of flesh and bone.

Theomania

*"From the very outset, then, 'Aurelia' seems to have been
strategically conceived by Nerval as a way of writing himself
out of captivity."*
                                        —Richard Sieburth

His madness for God
here and now,
in every wind and random light,
he believed
the world was dreaming him back,
all things in correspondent motion,
the night sky unfolding
like a final lover,
irradiating night to constellations
that reveal the real inside the unreal
unveiling silence into meanings
while alleys crooked with time and
poverty point a path to Saturn,
where all the green comes from,
and the stars cry out their names.
Through asylum windows
he watched his disinherited moon,
the night epitomized in pain
drawn from a bow.
He cannot get the doctors to see,
heaven hasn't got parts.
They released him when he agreed
to orphan all his visions.
When they finally found him,
strung like a bell from that lamppost,

slips of rhymed eternity
fluttered to wet streets
and stuck there,
waving in the wind
like pinned butterflies.

Such language

Welcome to Springview!
We're really glad you came—
(Write name here)
Sit back and peruse our brochure.
Look! Our campus is an "oasis,"
conveniently located
between Main Street and the Mall.
We hope you enjoy your stay!
Questions? Contact our Help Desk.
Observe our live birds kept in glass.
How beautiful—how calming their calls!
They sing like they know no other world.
That's a ping pong ball with a heart
dancing on our lobby fountain plume.
Such are our everyday miracles.
Won't you sign yourself in?
What was that? "The present's random demands"?
That is not on the form. Not sure what you mean.
Simply check all the appropriate boxes.
Please keep within the lines.
No smoking please.
Or drug use.
Just take this magic little pill
and all will be well.
You will be amazed
how long we can make you live,
an eternity bottled in days,
a remarkable quantity of life.
Excuse us?

"No word contains the silence"?
If you are asking for help, press the button.
Please cooperate. Niceness brings joy.

Now, now, no staring at old photographs.
No brooding alone. We have Scrabble, Bingo,
checkers and t.v.—and our popular specialty—
the required singalong.
Just think—
you might be here for a pleasant while.
Oh dear—(Write name here)—
Such language!

Hospice

The piano player has moved in for good.
His Steinway inhabits the lobby.
He's playing "Raindrops Keep Fallin' on my Head."
The desk is empty but for book and pen.
More than a few names means you're likely next.
No names means a little more time.
I pass each blue-glowing room—
TV and the dying—TV and the gone.
The walls weep antiseptics.
There's almost nothing left of my brother.
His cancer has hollowed him whole.
His bones are braced to whistle in the wind.
A voice: "Would your brother like a TV?"
No. "Many find it comforting." No.
Outside, someone is reading the sidewalk.
I have rehearsed this moment many times,
but now I've forgotten my lines. I sigh,
trying to remember a lifetime.
He whispers, "I'm cold," and with each blanket
I spread over him says, "Thank you. I'm cold."
A deep, abiding silence.
One more blanket for my brother.

The permeability of touch

An elderly couple
and I
pass on the sidewalk.
I nod, polite.
She stops, touches
my arm, and time shudders.
I have never seen them before.
She asks me three questions:
How have I been?
Why has it been so long?
How is my dear wife?
The man's eyes meet mine
in a silent language,
an agreement of fictions
too vital to question.
I take her hand,
fragile as a November leaf,
and speak my lines, improvising
a life I have never known.
They exit and I wonder
how a single touch
turns us into mysteries,
and loses our names in the stars.

The ancient fishermen

The ancient fishermen cast their lines
from boulders rolled here by centuries,
their heads nodding, lures nodding,
the light turned gold to silver in their hair.
They are as patient as the seasons
as they wait for the dark blue to speak,
as they wait for the tug deep below
that signals life and death, that brings
the fish that carry fire to the sun.

Death and only the lonely

To let words come falling like the faith of leaves,
to let things breathe and be--
This is when you learn to mold yourself
to chance occasions, unfolding into light.
This is when you let go all the dying.
And yet there comes a calling near,
not to write what you long for,
but for what longs for you
to speak it finally free, to try
to imagine it in return.
Like a madman confronts you in the street,
screaming that even death is holy, and all those
others in pain or silence, who break your heart
to beauty, teaching you to leave nothing out
alone and crying in the rain.

What I saw at the funeral home

I saw an acne-plagued boy
escort a rack of black suits
into a back room.
The suits were smooth, neatly-pressed,
prim as honored scholars,
each awaiting a future owner.
Our eyes met, and the boy's widened
in surprise, as if caught in the middle
of an inexplicable crime.
He seemed to me a sorcerer's apprentice,
glimpsed behind the magic curtain,
trying to sweep away the doom.
My altar-boy-God was a fierce old
Alchemist, with bloody eyes,
who changed base fear into faith.
But now I suspect God
in an aristocratic dowager,
with impeccable manners—
to have this many gentlemen callers.

Blessing the dead

It is easy to bless the dead,
as shyly as the moon surrenders her face,
or the half-closed eye of a dozing cat
inherits the darkness.
It is easy to remember the lost.
They tap at your window,
then send their sighs to the windy leaves
as they gently unwind the sun.
It is easy to touch words to silence.
It longs to listen for your longing
to seek a soul bound tight with wounds,
and make it lonely-wise.
It is easy to honor the dead.
It merely takes a gift for grieving,
distrust of self-appointed saints,
and a spoon for digging in the cold.

These days

Omen ash in air
rises to a blue ultimatum.
Why are my cries in the trees?
My nerve ends strung through the stars?
My heart listens to itself: these days.
The planets follow their gyroscope fates.
I watch them, trying to fall asleep,
cut flowers wilting in my eyes.
The daylight swallows its daily poison
and waits: Two times remain—the present
and an apocalypse of uncertain date
the size of a toy hat So these days
I watch for the minor wound that might
metastasize to calamity, the simple fall
that tumbles me through eternity,
and tempts the shadows creeping from the moon.
A scream comes out of a cloud,
but the sun is blind, the moon a deaf old man.
I'm brimful of song no one seems to hear.
It's curious how invisible you become—
a hand goes first, then a whole damn arm.
I may try whispering to total strangers,
helping them learn to see us both.

Facets of silence and memory

A sapphire despair
cut from the purity of loss,
facets of fear and memory,
this old age dug from the deep earth,
a world in one palm, blue-descending,
must mean something somewhere,
but nowhere has a chair in every room,
this fear has no face, stays silent
the way each star burns holes in the night,
and I misplace trifles and beloved people
that once held my past in place.
A diamond silence
dares the wind to recall its name,
but even echoes can't remember now
the cries of love that made them.
A silence so sure it can hear darkness grow
like skeletons in moonlight. Still, at times
I step clear from the present to one dear face
that flashes in a dream so pure and clear,
like fireflies held in a jar long ago,
then set free, set free, set free…

Elegy: What holds the eye now is what remembers

Well where have you been?
Those "felon winds" appear to have left us
for now, with all the other unversed mortals,
who merely ask for the right
to walk free in their own blessed skin,
unwounded by elegies that never heal.
The only words I need are here and now.
I'll make do with these, since the past
is a dream, the future a blank, and it's
no sin to keep on breathing when stars
fall to ashes, friends depart for parts unknown,
or words cling to some lost long-ago.
Nature forever sings us loss.
We poets invented nothing new.
Who do you want to be?
It might be just the bones you were born in.
It might be just the life you live, each day,
all your loving deeds that go unsung.
Step into your life, not some remembered
death. Step close, the rain comes now.
Like love, it needs no why. Like silence,
it asks no tribute. Like Spring, it needs
no tears to change it into green.

Plasto Man

Holy hell, I'm Plasto Man.
Molded my face from the sun
so I could become, become,
an undone geometry one.
I can mold my face
into any stranger I pass,
both the mask and the hidden,
the purity and the sin.
By sunset I've impersonated
half this dramatic town.
For encore I change blood to turnips,
and wounds to watches unwinding.
But my true superpower
is the way I make things up
and half believe them into truth,
till all villains are half-defeated,
justice nearly prevails,
and I can keep on dreaming.
You should see me masquerading
death, so purely he thinks he's
looking in a mirror, winks in self-
congratulation, flashes his strychnine
grin, and dances away, away, away…

Of a man skating

Once you were master of distance near,
equilibrium that balanced you whole,
the sound of your skates gliding diamond suns
to spin—then—stop, and feel the world
whirl round a prelude to your song, the high
notes pure decibels of your steel, carving
signatures of dream, then silence,
then the echoing woods.
You return now, all these years later,
hoping to find those echoes again,
but the time aches, the skates sting deep
and you are thinking—How retrace those
perfect, thoughtless patterns you wrote here
once, so long ago even the snowfall
can't remember? Perhaps no true echo
ever finds a home.
It is gone now, the forever circle
you might have only dreamed,
that encircled all the others, though
you still attempt the leap, hoping
time might collapse, fold up like
a pocket telescope. No. Divinity
never will be willed, and you must
learn to live in time and memory—
Here, where a teenage girl tries and tries,
awkward, chubby, flailing arms as she falls
and falls, picks herself up, curses, tries again,
tears trickling round her acne, the sky
an isolate darkness, but you can imagine

her grace matured, head far back, arms
in perfect equilibrium—someday—
spinning free in starlit joy.

Enquento

So blue it could be Varo's dream-mirror,
you in the center of this frozen pond,
alone in the purity of ice.
Now you see your original face,
the one from before you were born,
looking back at you looking back.
The footing seems sound, yet you
have chosen this earth-mirror from others
less perilous of descent.
Now you hear a whispered crack, like
the sound of a sparrow's back snapped,
and your mirror shatters into swords
that wound you to meanings you never knew
before, shredding your nerve ends and you
splinter and fall through the earth down into
darkness with secrets to tell, perhaps
the silence that devours pain, in depths
unfathomed, you trace the depths of fear.
If you stay here you will die, but if you claw
your way back to the light, you may become
a graceful skater of perils, signing your name
in tragic glass.

Kaleidoscope of mirrors

Hand are rules
here
your hands will teach you
visions are physical,
require turning and returning,
selves and un-selves,
to find another new.
Soundless carousel
spinning the colors of the wind,
whirling dull white of heaven
to stained glass purity of earth,
cool as an empty church.
Listening mirrors
each
subverting the reflection
before, each image
dispelled, re-played,
sung to rainbows
by the next wanded magic
we misspell as everyday.
Blue to silver, silver to glass
of constellations,
freed from fate and memory,
gently folding and unfolding worlds
that long to speak the light.
Is it random chance
that redreams all the colors,
or conspiracy of hand and eye?
Or do the images arrive

of their own chosen whim,
like Autumn winds
spinning their gold from green?

Who could have guessed
a single turn
could overturn a universe?
And though it may wound you
to let some worlds go
like butterflies climbing to the sun,
you must keep turning or die.

Three times not to die

Past
Fireflies—here—there—
gold rings on ebony silk—
bind light and dark
silence and memory,
as if they came
to heal the night's wounds,
suturing them with suns,
rendering them back to whole
So compass my heart
to memory,
the way my mother still
sways gently in her summer swing,
reading Rimbaud to the winds.

Present
Could you have predicted
the way this child hides
her tears inside her sleeve?
Each day is its own
ars poetica

Future
Teach me to converse with the weeds.
Lay me here unfolding in your arms.
Here where moonlight bewilders the trees,
and love is hallowed in flesh and bone
until the wind learns to speak our names.

Rules of Retirement

I

When descending
into a dungeon,
be sure to carry a shovel

II

In case you were wondering,
you must
descend to this dungeon.

III

Dig until daylight
shimmers free, then
abandon the shovel.

IV

Pull yourself from this tomb of time.
There is still a world to learn,
no matter how late or uncertain.

V

Now leaves share their gold with you
in random signatures of love,
clouds alone-ing in morning blue.

It

Pull it from a silence,
urge it to a witness,
hear it to a testament,
confess it to heaven or hell.
Seed it to the earth,
tremble it into flower,
swell it to a ripeness,
pregnant with possibility.
Carve it to a clarity,
sand it smooth as stone,
rub it in longing to endure the night,
and speak the spirit free.
Flame it to a white heat,
hammer it with thunder,
weld it sure with lightning,
baptize it with storm.
Bold it to a sunburst,
polish it to a moon,
unfold it like a universe,
web it round with stars.
Then it will be good
to eat, drink, house, heal,
ride, soar, sail, explore
for a million's million years—or more.

Rain I don't mind

Rain winding unpre-
dictable lines or streams
or rivers the width of
a fingernail
down a windowpane re-
fute metaphysics, re-
veal the process is
itself the pattern,
randoming into thought, re-
vealing more than any mirror,
unraveling into a form
all its own, a sort of
prayer, seeking for one
lonely chance to complete the union
of time and vision.

Renga in Gold, White, Blue and Green

Gold leaves weaving
their random fates
scatter all philosophy
never learns
what the wind
knows
the language
of trees
embracing light
reveals the blue
city is absence
the lost excluded
middles
have a way
of returning
the darkness
teaching tombstones
to whisper
silence
emptying words
return us to touch
the world calls to us
in winds
to render it whole again
a heart breaks
to bind the scattered
stars

singing light
deep
into our veins

comes the pulsing
green
of Saturn
might be
where angels go
when they finally learn to love
we may chant to God
upon our dying:
Hold me like a child dreaming through your eyes

Light and silence

A honeybee's hum
disturbs the universe
and
the swallow
touches a celandine
to light and silence
is loss,
is loss embodied
in time
dies
when the light dies
and silence listens in the dark
dreams never
realize in words,
cannot preserve time
is light, is light
moving in silence
is memory, is memory
unravels
into time,
into mystery
remains always,
knows only
a lost embrace
must be
how death feels,
and thus begins desire

to live
if only as
a cherry's ripening blood

wants what it wants,
wants silence and light,
yet to hear the pulse
of all longing
is blind
to the angels
descend
only
when heaven is empty
the mind
to silence,
to light remembering
how the colors
once possessed
more than just their names
only pin the butterfly,
never free it
to light and silence
the darkness that screams,
that refuses to accept
that even loneliness is holy
life the secret we all must learn,
holy the swallow singing the silence,
holy the honey bee engoldening the light.

Autumn leaving

Each falling leaf refutes Plato,
the way silver dandelions
seed the random winds with song.
Watch now as a leaf
ignites the flame
of its only freedom
composing the Fall
in light
and motion
and this wind believes
it once knew you long ago,
casting its gold through trembling air.
And suddenly your whole life seems
to have been silently, confusedly, yet
lovingly arranged, like a mother trying
to straighten her teenager's room, no
divine plan, but you'll find what you need
there, in her ramshackled good intentions.
Pain neatly folded and shut in drawers,
contained, since it never leaves on its own.
Loss and mystery stored in the closet,
for future use in memory, while outside
your winedark window, Autumn leaves
speak to your willing heart
of other worlds whispering round the stars,
and whisper it will soon be time to go.

How the moon inhabits time

Moon and wind, westering their secrets.
When did midnight learn to use a knife?
We know the darkness of pain and loss,
but what lies beyond the restful silence?
Each night the sky unveils its wounded stars.
By day we trace the green-song
casting its music through the air,
and yet the roots go where the mind cannot,
and we are left questioning the surface,
and learn no depths beyond our shallow graves.
Yet, so long as my words unfold
the voice of another's longing,
or capture a mother's elusive song
to herself, her child, or the moon,
I may agree to live another day.
God grant me time to affirm both dark and light,
sun, moon, star, even the void between,
until I have memorized each flight and fall,
until I have finally learned to bless
all the colors of mortality.